Ahlumba Harris

Morning Cup of Jo

Ahlumba Harris

Morning Cup of Jo
Inspiration Brings Life

AHLUMBA HARRIS

To order additional copies of this book, contact:

Inspired2Prosper International LLC
P.O Box 504 Union City, GA 30291
contactus@inspired2prosper.com
www.inspired2prosper.com
www.ahlumba.com

DEDICATION

Robert Harris and Barber Zeigler though I did not have the best childhood I still remembered thanking the Lord for giving me to you both, for the foundation of greatness I have stems from you both.

CONTENTS

ACKNOWLEDGMENTS

Of course none of this would have been possible without my Lord and Savior Jesus Christ! As always Aniyla you are my shining light. Bahia, Malika, Gibran, Christie, Yetmon, Ladipo, and Tonya you all are awesome and I love you like blood…Oh you are blood…lol. Andy Monk I have to thank you for the beautiful book cover you designed for my book. You successfully captured the essence of what I was going for. Most importantly I thank you the reader for allowing Morning Cup of Jo to be a part of your day!

Ahlumba Harris

PROLOGUE

SEASONS OF CHANGE

Hearing from God each day has this uncanny ability to energize, give clarity in the areas we lack understanding, and provides us with the strength needed to accomplish our next level of greatness. I liken this to inspiration. I believe inspiration to be intangible and unexplainable, for one can be inspired be anything whether it be the beauty of a day, an object seen in passing, a person's words, a book, or even life itself. The wonder that we can be encouraged by anything that connects to us during a moment of need is amazing. We are all somehow connected through our struggles and the desire to have purpose.

Encouragement is important for in our daily walk we all will encounter some degree of adversity. At times due to fear we give the weight of our difficulty so much authority that we allow it to dictate life decisions. As a result we lie defeated, so scared of the struggle that we might incur on ourselves that we willingly embrace a life less than; a life of mediocrity. The word of God never said that we would be trouble free but that we would be troubled on every side yet not distressed; that we would be perplexed, but not in despair. Persecuted, but not forsaken; cast down, but not destroyed.

When in pursuit of any great thing hardship will come but the Lord has equipped us with the wares to handle it. When one is inspired the seed of hope, possibility, expectation, belief, and optimism becomes planted in the individual. Though once downtrodden he or she now has the renewed faith needed to continue pressing towards the dream, vision, or goal they thought to be impossible.

In life we all have or will encounter the positive and negative change that comes with living, for each level achieved it becomes a necessity to go through a different season of your life.

Just as the earth goes through its transition of change so will you. In our everyday walk we experience the various stages of life based off the current season we are experiencing.

There are seasons of lack, seasons of increase, and seasons of loneliness which all serve a purpose of growth. Just as the planet orbits the sun we are orbiting life itself. At times you will experience some of your darkest days as in winter or the bright newness of a new day that can only be swept in like the first day of summer; which just so happens to usher in the most abundance of sunlight…i.e. joy and increase you have ever experienced.

Out of my own pain, struggle and desire for more I realized that Inspiration Brings Life. This book is intended to inspire, encourage, and uplift you as you go through your season of change and pursue the different levels of greatness by way of providing thirty days of quotes, short stories, antidotes, and/or scriptures to support, give confidence, and promote positive growth, for we overcome by the telling of our testimonies.

Why thirty days of Inspiration? Well, It has been said that it takes up to thirty days to form a new habit however I tend to find myself on the fence as it relates to that theory. On the other hand I believe that thirty days of consistency is a great start to establishing a new beginning. By creating a stable pattern of consistency you have proven to yourself that you do have the ability to focus on and achieve a task therefore allowing the self assurance in your ability and readiness to take it to its next level.

There comes a time when one must stop planning and eventually do. In order to make your way prosperous you must first put forth some action. The only way to change your tomorrow is by doing something different today!

For the next thirty days as you read this book I challenge you to breathe life back into your God given dream, vision, or goal. Get up and not only pursue but obtain that long awaited, only dreamed of, thought to be impossible aspiration that you willingly allowed to corrode in a crevice never to see the light of day.

Greatness is in you raging for that one opportunity to be unrestricted. Free yourself and make your way prosperous!

STICK WITH IT

DAY 1

"God calls you for what you will be, not what you currently are..."

In the moments when the journey to build something better for yourself and/or family becomes a little difficult to bear, don't give up, but be encouraged for nothing worth having was ever built in a day! The most successful businessman, entertainer, educator, or even the inanimate object you sit on had a beginning.

No matter your degree of living, whether it be grandiose, lackluster or bottom of the barrel everyone or thing had to first be established from somewhere. What you may consider to be a hindrance, setback, and/or difficulty today will become your unexpected character builder of tomorrow. Do not allow what you perceive to be a problem obstruct your path to success. Lack, drug abuse, weight, health issues or a learning disability should never be given the determining power on what can or cannot be achieved in your life. Don't look at your circumstance instead take the small steps needed to change your tomorrow.

I can identify with your desire for more, your struggle, dreams unattained, loss, and despair. It is my belief that if you stop allowing the excuses and the fear that stricken your growth from continuing to prevent the expansion of your dream, vision, or goal you then will allow God the freedom to lay out the path to a greater tomorrow.

Always believe in yourself and the God given dream, vision, or goal He has impregnated you with. Keep going until you birth it and I can almost guarantee that every struggle of your past will truly be worth the struggle compared to the reward you will receive.

NEVER GIVE UP!

DAY 2

"Through my tears and fears of the unknown on whether I will succeed or fail, I am determined to continue to move forward. When it rains, it does pour, but rain helps to bring in your harvest..."

Having a wonderful vision for your life is not hard. From childhood, we allowed ourselves the freedom to dream and believe that anything we wanted in life was possible. A child, unashamedly with boldness, states everything they will accomplish in their future without taking into account the journey that it will take to get there. It is important to have that childlike belief in your ability, but with the added knowledge and wisdom that vitality, strength of mind, health, and spirit is needed, that you girt yourself for the journey ahead.

I remember this great desire I had to own my own home. I wanted a house so badly I would sit back while HGTV played in the background and daydream about it. One day I finally made the decision to do what was needed so that I could achieve the long awaited goal of homeownership. Never would I have imagined that the process would take almost three and a half years. It was one of the most mentally and spiritually draining moments of my life.

For over two years my daughter and I slept on the floor in the living room of a family member's apartment. For two years I ate humble pie; for over two years I felt less than adequate; for over two years I constantly asked the Lord "why?". Sure, I was working towards something, but that meant nothing when there was no end in sight nor any proof that it would ever happen.

Daily I would tell my daughter "One day we will have our house, one day you will have your own room," but our one day never seemed to come. Days turned into weeks, weeks turned into months, and months into years.

On the verge of giving up and prepared to throw in the towel, I made peace with the decision to live in an apartment when the Lord offered me an olive branch by way of a call from my counselor. He stated the following "We were able to get you pre-qualified. Can you come in today to get your letter?" Joy and happiness are words that will never fully describe the explosion that being pre-qualified created in me. The day I longed for, for what seemed to be an eternity was beginning to happen.

On September 11th, 2012, I who never lived in a house, became a proud homeowner. I, who never owned much of anything, but debt and bad credit was able to win the over two year battle. I, who always said "One day," was finally able to say "Today." Remain the course and the pursuit of your dream. I am a living testament that if you never give up on your quest for more, your "one day" will eventually be... Today!

GO THE EXTRA MILE

DAY 3

"Fight for your success. To give up welcomes defeat but in holding on just a while longer, you allow room for your latter to be greater..."

One week while out jogging, a man from across the street hollered to me, "You're almost there, don't give up you're almost there," not knowing that I had just started. But, in just beginning I already looked worn out and tired; yet I still had the entire work out ahead of me. However, thanks to those words of encouragement, I was no longer filled with the trepidation of not wanting to work-out, but given the focus needed to stay the course and before I knew it I was almost there...finished.

How often in life do we go through something, see no end in sight and wonder; Will I ever make it? Imagine the devastation of stopping one step shy of your victory. To give up welcomes defeat, but in holding on a little longer you allow room for your latter to be greater. Sometimes we stay strong for so long that the drain of doing the right thing with no end in sight becomes tiresome.

Do not let dread get in the way of your potential. Be encouraged today and keep going. For no matter what stage of the journey, trial, struggle, and/or hardship you are currently in, allow these next four words to soak into your consciousness "You are Almost There!"

BE BOLD AND CROSS YOUR OCEAN

DAY 4

"Gather the confidence needed to walk outside of the area that brings you comfort ...lest you never realize the potential of what could have been..."

Often times we allow the vision we have for our future to slip right through our fingertips, fall to the ground, and be buried with the sorrows of un-fulfillment. There will never be an ideal situation or time to achieve goals. Instead of fighting for the reason why you can achieve the success you once envisioned for your life, you now constantly find one excuse or one reason after another on why your goals are not possible.

Ideally, we all would prefer that all of our ducks were all lined in a perfect little row before taking the steps down a road that is unfamiliar. No matter how desperately you wish that they were, it is not possible to control the unplanned things that arise in life. However, if not careful, it can be used to deter you.

Do not allow the fear you have of the lack of control over life's circumstances stop you from stepping out of your comfort zone. Have faith in yourself and God's ability to protect you, for we are all awesome in our own right. Fight for your success, pursue your dream and make it a reality. No matter the circumstances you currently face, be determined to overcome. Rise up and be inspired to prosper.

WHAT MAN DENIES GOD APPROVES

DAY 5

"The pain of your situation may overwhelm you to tears but don't fret for water brings in the harvest..."

God does not care about your credit, where you have been, or what you used to represent. Once you have sought forgiveness he no longer sees the sin of your past, but the brightness of your future. The heart of man is not determined by his credit, his worth, or his know how, but somehow we have fallen victim to believing that our merit lies in whether or not we are approved.

In today's society being approved is big business. We are approved for apartments, cars, credit cards, bank accounts, and insurance. Almost everything in this world requires a degree of approval to achieve success. I was once denied so often that I began to deny myself. I believed my value to be based on whether or not man accepted me.

Be free from the conformities of this world; for God will not only take you as you are but increase you where you stand without any strings attached. Liberate yourself from the shackles and hurt of disapproval, for what God offers is a sweat-less victory that is free of charge.

FULFILL YOUR DESTINY

DAY 6

"Don't try to short cut your way to success; Step up and be the change that you hope someone else will initiate..."

Often we want to make a change in this world, yet due to laziness we ignore the tasks needed to be completed with the hope that someone else will step up and handle it. If you ever become aware of a problem, don't wait for someone else to fix it, step up to the plate and change it because the next person that comes along might also choose to pass the buck leaving the issue unresolved.

One day while traveling down the road, I noticed that ever since I began this new route, the pedestrian signal at the intersection of Joseph E Boone and West Lake Avenue never worked. The first time I saw it, I paused and thought "hmm the light is out," the second time I thought "well I'm sure somebody else will call it in," the third time I was like "okay I need to call and get this fixed," but to no avail for they were just residing thoughts with no action. It was not until I passed the intersection for the fourth time that I finally stopped and determined to myself that I would not put this off again for yet another day.

Hence, I called the Atlanta Traffic Control Center and by the fifth day it was up and running smoothly allowing the pedestrians the opportunity to yet again cross the street safely. I do not know how long that intersection was inoperable before I came along; but what I do know is that it did not get fixed until I made up in my mind to do what I could to make it better. Stop waiting on someone else to do something for you. Don't spend your life waiting on someone else to do what you can do for yourself.

DON'T SETTLE

DAY 7

"In choosing to live a less than capable existence, you are willingly limiting the greatness dwelling within..."

What are you waiting for? Do not allow another year to pass without ever taking any real action towards living your life or making your dream a reality. Unless you have achieved everything then this does not pertain to you but if you are one of the millions out there who has something missing and un-fulfilled then it is time for you to put your faith into action, it is time to believe in yourself, and it is time to trust that the Lord has your back.

Do not fight to keep your limitations! Although you have all the rationale, explanations, and facts at the ready on why it can't be done, I implore you to unearth the one reason that makes it a possibility; in doing so you are taking your single step to a better tomorrow.

Stop waiting and release the Kraken within you! Otherwise continue to live a contained mediocre life with nothing to chew on but lost dreams and hopes.

SELF WORTH

DAY 8

"You must first believe before anyone else accepts your potential as true. Today, walk in confidence for you are worthy, capable, and competent!"

It is important to always keep a positive view of yourself. I have noticed that when one's life is in shambles by no fault of their own they start to doubt their own ability. When you don't believe in yourself it becomes almost impossible to advance any real growth in your life due to the feelings of unworthiness

There was a time in my life when I was beginning to lose all hope and belief in any potential I thought I had. I was just barely holding on with a hope and a dream when something happened that almost broke me. I wrote a post on my twitter account that read, "Have hope when you have no reason to hope." Un-expectantly someone responded with "How does one believe when they have no reason to?"

To my dismay, I could not answer that question. For at that very moment I was going through a struggle that had been ongoing for the past two years and if I was to tell the truth, I was losing my faith, my way, and my belief. With no answer and that question dangling in my head I had no choice but to take a second look at myself.

I contemplated how could I continue to give the advice to keep pushing, hang in there, yada, yada, yada, the same old nonsense everybody tells everybody when I no longer wanted to keep pushing, when I myself was barely able to believe. Those thoughts left me even more unnerved. More doubtful in my ability to achieve than ever, I sunk deeper in the pool of torment I created for myself. I began to believe that unimaginable success and wealth was an unattainable mirage only meant for the select few.

As a result, I pushed back from 12p; which was what I believed to be my purpose, and searched myself. Somewhere along the way I allowed my faith, trust, and belief in God's ability to falter. Though I was hurting, lonely, and at times a little scared deep down I knew God favored me. I slowly came to terms with the fact that if I did not believe in myself and my potential no one would.

No matter the peril I encountered, it was imperative that I trusted God's ability to guide me through. So on faith I pushed myself to not look at what I lacked because if I did not, those thoughts of failure and defeat would hound me yet again. I refused to allow the struggle of my yesterday to be a continuation of my tomorrow.

There will come several instances in your life when you must motivate yourself while staying confident in your ability to deliver the goods even when it seem as if you have none.

With the pressure to succeed on your back, God is able to give you the peace you lack while renewing and reinforcing the confidence missing in your ability, your purpose, and your current role in life.

Just because things are not currently what you hoped it to be, don't lose sight of the greatness that is in you. If you have no faith in yourself, how can you be successful? Your ability to believe in yourself is at times determined by the way you view yourself.

HARD WORK EQUALS SUCCESS

DAY 9

"It's not enough to hope for a change if you are unwilling to exercise the self control while putting forth the action needed to successfully achieve what seemed to be the impossible..."

We are all building towards something greater; one step at a time. Sometimes the road to making it a reality is not always evident by way of a yellow brick road, but it is more like a brick wall blocking your path. Success and opportunity is all around us by way of television, magazines, internet, and books to name a few.

The desire to underestimate the requirement of hard work should never be acted upon, for it is the only given to realizing your success.

Unfortunately, besides hard work, persistence, perseverance, and faith, there is no clear concise formula to obtaining success because it happens differently for everyone.

Talent alone does not equal success, education alone does not equal success, diet alone does not equal success, but your ability paired with hard work multiplied by perseverance equals your opportunity…

Don't give up on your dream because of its difficulty!

GOOD HEALTH

DAY 10

Why are you so selfish with your smile? Why are you so tight with your wave? Does kindness bring you such pain? Maybe if you smiled you would not be so enraged...

According to Acts 20:35, "It is more blessed to give than to receive," but giving does not always entail the exchange of money. Sometimes it is as simple as gracing someone with a smile or giving them a compliment.

At times we take for granted that what is simple for one is simple for all. Be willing to help others attain their goal. Who knows while aiding another, you might un-expectantly reach your own!

So today, choose to give because you never know how your small gesture of kindness could uplift a person who is in need of it.

LET GO OF YOUR WORRIES

DAY 11

"Wait on the Lord be of good courage and he shall strengthen your heart: wait I say on the Lord...Psalms 27:14"

When the road to success becomes too hard to bear, remember your faith and the enthusiasm you once had. Difficult times will arise and hard choices will be made; however keep in mind that the weightier the obstacle the greater the potential victory...

Yes, sometimes it is hard to wait on the Lord when you are going through. You want the pain to stop now, the struggle to end now, the success to happen now, the relationship now, the hurt to subside now. But I have learned the hard way that sometimes you have to patiently endure today before you can receive what you have been promised.

Don't wait until you see the evidence of increase before you are cheerful, but take a stand and have that joy despite your circumstances!

So I encourage you, just as I needed encouragement, to stay

the course. Choose not to fear your current circumstances for the Lord is your present help.

PRESS YOUR WAY

DAY 12

"No matter what you aspire to be, great or small, the support you yearn for will eventually come. But sometimes there is a need to soldier on for yourself by yourself..."

If support and acceptance from the masses was easy, it would not be a novelty to have it. What I have learned is that people will reject you. Support is not easily attained and hard work is a necessity. But in spite of that it is important to remain at peace with yourself. Do not take offense because of the lack of understanding that others may have as it relates to your dream, vision, or the path you have chosen, for everything is not for everyone. Most importantly don't reject yourself. Instead reject the desire to allow your fear of what others might say or your fear of failure to outweigh your desire to succeed.

I longed to be able to help those in need in a way that was not made available for me. Because of fear, I almost decided not to pursue my passion, I tried to dampen the desire I had to help others. I knew that I wanted to make a positive difference but I thought, "Who would want to listen to me, I am nobody." Despite my doubts I had a little light to guide me. So, I began writing which eventually turned into a book. Then I started a business, which stemmed from a deeply rooted desire I had to become an inspirational speaker (amongst other things). Due to my lack of finances I did not have a clear picture of how to accomplish my goals.

Eventually I was made aware of the plethora of free business tools at my disposal which afforded me the opportunity to create a business website and several social media pages. Excited, I believed that my business success was as simple as the line from the movie Field of Dreams, "If you build it they will come." Boy was I wrong!

It was hard getting the support that I thought would be freely given. My confidence was constantly shaken due to the lack of response and lack of interest. Daily, I battled with the desire to give up. The rejection I felt was like a blow to the gut. It overwhelmed me. I began to doubt myself, my dreams, and my path. I was unsure of myself. constantly I played with the idea of giving up but what would I have then.

Today, I thank God that I did not give up. At the beginning of anything new you will experience difficulty, but it is your responsibility to dig deep down in yourself and remember why you were doing it in the first place.

ACHIEVABLE DOABLE THEREFORE POSSIBLE

DAY 13

"Success and prosperity is not evident just through financial wealth, but also through the accomplishment of being able to overcome any hindering obstacle in your life by making a positive change..."

I once thought that my business worth was contingent upon the number of likes, followers, or comments I received but I have since realized that it is so much more than that. It transcends into my conversations, my daily walk and the impact I make each day in the lives of those around me.

I thank God for revelation and for the willingness to be a vessel of positive change. If by chance, my current or past experiences in life have the ability to touch someone today for the better, then I know what I strive to achieve daily is not in vain.

When doubt tries to overtake your mind with thoughts of why your dream, vision, or goal is unattainable, shut it down with a resounding "It is already done!"

LIVE LIFE

DAY 14

Stop working and enjoy the fruits of your labor or be in danger of losing what you were doing it for...

Do you sometimes find yourself in a bad place mentally because you are so busy taking care of everything and everyone else that you forget your own-self? Choose to be remembered today! Whether or not you have achieved the level of success you had hoped for, it is important that you find time to enjoy the fruits of your labor.

Stop and relish moments that life has to offer for they are priceless seconds in time that can never be returned unto you. Treat yourself, take your family and experience the joy and fun that only living in the now can offer.

HOLD YOUR CALM

DAY 15

"As the tempest of doubt and trouble rage around you, remember that even while in the mist of your dilemma therein still lie a place of solace..."

Many people take the steps to making their dream a reality, but hundreds possibly thousands end the journey prematurely due to unforeseen difficulties. Don't give up when you have gone so far!

On several occasions I wanted to end my journey to financial freedom. But to give up, would mean a never ending life of, No not today, I can't, I don't have, and I need.

When it seems as if the thing you are pressing for is ever out of your reach to the point of you welcoming defeat, revive your dream, vision, or goal by remembering why you were pursuing it in the first place. There is peace in the eye of the storm!

No matter what difficulty, pain, or hardship you may be experiencing, remember troubles don't last always. Just like the raging storm that soon subsides, allow the uproar of your heart to settle into a place of peace. For this too shall pass...

Morning Cup of Jo

I DON'T KNOW- BUT I DO- I DO- BUT I DON'T!

DAY 16

"Don't settle for a life of less than enough. Remember the forgotten ambitions of your past and say aloud, "it's still possible." You must first have the courage to believe so that you can later achieve...."

Have you ever had the attack of the indecisive? It becomes a terrible tug of war when your heart wants to go in one direction and your mind is leading you down another. Sometimes we just need to pull the trigger. Stop riding the fence; be it hot or cold, choose one because in most cases lukewarm is not an option.

The moment you allow your faith to falter you give room for doubt and negative reasoning to enter. Do not allow the smokescreen of failure to tempt you into releasing what you have labored so long to achieve before you even receive the manifestation of it...

SOMETIMES IT PAYS TO BE IRRITATED

DAY 17

"Often we look at the struggles that come against us as a fate worse than. Not realizing that sometimes we have to go through the process of pain to produce the end result of greatness!"

Have you ever seen or admired the beauty of a natural pearl? Have you ever wondered how such a beautiful thing was created? Amazingly enough that beautiful pearl in all its splendor is only manifested after it has exerted an unwanted, unsolicited stream of aggravation to its carrier.

The carrier...i.e. the clam is first irritated by a speck of sand. As a means of defense it creates a fluid to rid or protect itself from the intrusion. The clam never gives up on trying to free its shell of the sand. All along the clam continues to produce layer upon layer of this fluid, which is deposited over the speck of sand until a beautiful pearl is formed.

It pays to be irritated so don't be dismayed by what appears to be your down fall. For achievement has this uncanny way of biting you in the rear when you least expect it...

GREAT THINGS HAS SMALL BEGINNINGS

DAY 18

"To loath, look down upon, or spurn your humble beginnings is to hinder your own journey to success..."

Every now and then it is important to remember where we come from to appreciate where we currently are. As in anything that we struggle with, the achievement of greatness is a everyday walk. When we falter or fall, it is imperative that we get back up and continue moving forward because the reward is in the journey not necessarily in the arrival.

Sure, we all want more out of life and rightly so, but it is important to be thankful for the little things while walking in expectation of the greatness to come. Pray that the Lord renews your mind and give thanks for your hardship because for everything there is a season.

DON'T DO IT

DAY 19

"Do not fall victim to the temptation of gossip. To find joy in another's struggle by way of discussing it with another besides the one going through it delays your own development..."

Although gossip has this innocent way of sliding into our daily conversation, you still have the choice to be great not small and ignore the hearsay. An individual that idly stands by to enjoy the suffering of someone else's personal or professional hardship is one with low character.

Gossip destroys relationships. Anxiety, lack of trust, hurt feelings, and low self esteem are some things that result from gossip. Therefore, be mindful of the next time someone approaches you with the new batch of rumors fresh out of the oven because the next time it could be you getting baked.

OUTLOOK MATTERS

DAY 20

"Do not allow the trials, hardship, and difficulties of life to frustrate your mental capacity to function. For it's not your problems that stop you, but your approach to handling them..."

During the pursuit of any new endeavor, you are bound to experience difficulties that cloak themselves as failures. But allow it to be a stimulant not a deterrent, for with determination and perseverance you and success will one day collide. The pain of your situation may overwhelm you to tears but don't fret for rain brings in the harvest. Have faith in your ability to succeed, for you are awesome in your own right. Be fearless, pursue your dream and make it a reality.

As you journey to attain spiritual, mental, physical, or financial success you then set in motion the onslaught of knowledge. With that onslaught; growth, development, progress, and evolution of character becomes an inevitable end result.

.

TROUBLE DON'T LAST ALWAYS

DAY 21

"Come unto me, all ye that labour and are heavy laden, and I will give you rest..."~Matthew 11:28 KJV

There is no need to carry what is not yours to bear. Yes, struggles of any kind are a heavy burden, but in releasing the weight of lack, fear,
uncertainty, personal battles, or relationship woes, you allow our
Lord, the Prince of Peace, room to enter in and have his perfect work...

It is hard to stand powerlessly by when the limitation of your resources restrict the fulfillment of a dream. But in your ability to rise above the justification of "can't," you then make peace with your humble beginnings by working within your means, thereby welcoming greatness.

Therefore, do not succumb to the hopelessness that uncertainty breeds, but have the courage to believe beyond the fear that will try to beset you.

Perfection has only been attained by one so do not allow what you do not have or need to stop you from taking the action needed to achieve your goals.

ORDINARY IS FOR THE BIRDS

DAY 22

"Do not allow the lack of vision that uncertainty creates hinder you from your appointed destiny..."

In choosing to break from the norm, one will garner disapproval. For it is virtually impossible to satisfy every person you encounter. However, the more difficult the struggle becomes, stand strong, face the firing squad, and achieve your goals or fruitlessly be a people pleaser and have nothing.

In choosing to live a less than capable existence, you willingly limit the greatness dwelling within. Do not let fear get in the way of your potential. In today's society, "be realistic" is said habitually to anyone who wants to step out on faith and make the dream a reality. But is it realistic to welcome lack? Is it sensible to embrace hardship? Is there truly practicality in suffering?

Awaken the innovator in you and flush realistic down the toilet. Be willing to free yourself from the fear of failure and what others may think of you. Revive the gifts and talents that you once hindered from growing.

Though the idea of failure has the ability to cause some to bury their desire to attain success, to cage aspiration is almost likened unto a fate worse than death. Free yourself from the bondage of fear. While in the mist of hard times don't give up, for it always appears worst than it really is. Hold on and refuse to resign yourself to failure...

SPEAK LIFE

DAY 23

"A man's belly shall be satisfied with the fruit of his mouth; and with the increase of his lips shall he be filled..."
~ Proverbs 18: 20

On the road to a better you, fear will come knocking, choose not to embrace it like a friend long lost but confront it head on and become fearless. Failure should never be an option. Do not discount what seems to be the impossible. For with a little confidence in yourself and the yearning for something better, you will be amazed by what you can achieve.

Your abundance or the lack there of is attracted by the words you allow to come out of your mouth. Despite the fact that negativity is more accepted, in order to have something different you must do something different. Always keep in mind you have what you say you have; therefore speak joy not pain, love not hate, and life not death...

BUT I AM AFRAID

DAY 24

"Despite your fear, take the leap of faith, and do it afraid under the guise of confidence; while being assured that all things work together for the Good of those who love the Lord..."

Life is a journey of daily steps. If you are willing to go the distance, you will be amazed by the leaps and bounds you have already taken. I remember being afraid to write because I thought I could not. I remember sitting on the patio outside the apartment door wondering would I ever possess my own home. I remember the destitute of nothingness. But the word of God says "weeping may endure for a night, but joy comes in the morning." Every day that I am blessed to wake up, I experience my morning!

The traditional job does not guarantee success, but because it is the conventional route most are encouraged to take it. However, there will come a time(in order to thrive and reach a higher level of achievement) that you will be required to go beyond the norm by taking the path less traveled.

If we are doomed to be afraid, then why not be afraid while doing something worth being afraid of! If we are going to have doubts, why not have doubts while facing something that seems impossible; and if lack insists on knocking at the door, why not give it a run for its money because this dream that you have will become a full reality!

RELEASE

DAY 25

"Sometimes you have to laugh to keep from crying, then again there's nothing wrong with a good cry..."

Sometimes when you are going through something it feels as if you will never get over it. But it is important to trust God, for he will never lead you astray. So go ahead and cry with the knowledge that this journey before you   will not be made alone for the Lord said, "I will never leave you nor forsake you."

Therefore, when the pain of your today becomes too much to bear, by all means cry and release the sorrow that is trying to beset and overcome you. For even in the midst of your sadness you can still have inner peace.

HOW BAD DO YOU WANT IT

DAY 26

The seed of greatness is in you! Neither lack, homelessness, nor the crab mentality of others have the power to hinder, slow down, or stop what God has in store for you.

When looking impossibility straight in the eye, it becomes difficult to stay the course of achieving your goals. It causes you to doubt that the gift in you was truly a gift. You begin to wonder, "is it really possible for me to continue my education, purchase my own house, build a successful business, lose this weight, or was I fooling myself the entire time?"

In order to make the dream a reality, almost every successful person had to persevere while experiencing the fears and doubts of "what if." You are not the lone ranger; difficulty did not begin with you. Take courage in knowing that there are several men and women out there who are currently fulfilling their destiny who once felt the same emotions that try to terrorize you.

When thoughts of uncertainty bombard you, take heart in knowing that there once was a time when impossible stared down those whom we now consider to be great. They too had to keep going when they probably would have preferred the ease of sailing on smooth waters versus the turmoil that came with creating a new path.

Greatness is in you. Give it room to bloom and allow it to break free!

BE THANKFUL

DAY 27

"I was desperate for something; So I prayed for anything; But once I received it; I found reason to complain; I got what I asked for but now I'm in pain; the very thing I thought I wanted has changed..."

Sometimes the thing you want the most will probably be the least likely to bring the wholeness desired for your life. Out of the desperation of our need, we sometimes make rash decisions. The anxiety caused at the thought of the possibility of never achieving can cause a certain level of unrest. Unrest causes turmoil and turmoil causes a lack of happiness.

As a result, you begin to labor for something while constantly pushing off your joy for later. Stop and relish the moment! Do not withhold your joy for the one day that you hope to have everything. Instead enjoy every step of your journey with the added delight that greater is in store.

PERCEPTION IS EVERYTHING

DAY 28

"Continue to press ahead knowing that every step forward is a victory..."

Discerning the correct path for your life will not always be an easy task. It will sometimes require you to make painful decisions. Despite the complexity of the choices you will have to make, continue to trust God and before you know it your opportunity will seize you!

Be ever so mindful of the choices you make for in your choices is the ability to determine the end result of your future. No matter what path you choose, difficulty will arise; but it is important that you stay your course and don't give up. For the suffering of your today will surely be worth the magnificence of your tomorrow.

FACE YOUR FEAR

DAY 29

"Don't despair when man tries to label you because of your appearance...for the Lord sees not as man sees; while man attempts to judge your worth based on your outward appearance, the Lord looks at your heart..."

As a result of the uncertainty that fear attracts, lack of vision becomes inevitable. Do not fall prey to the consequences of fear instead challenge yourself to carry out a task that once caused you trepidation.

Trouble is a distraction that obstructs your potential success; however, in pressing past the difficulty that arises, you will be surprised by the strength that's in you to overcome and accomplish a feat you once assumed to be beyond your reach.

Force yourself to take the small baby steps and one day when you turn around you will see the long strides already taken. Therefore, realizing that the power that you gave to your fear was unwarranted.

YOU CAN'T STOP NOW

DAY 30

"Despite opposition, therein still lies a purpose..."

It's never the end just the beginning of a new season. Trouble comes to detour and discourage you from reaching your appointed destiny. Sometimes while in the midst of hurt, pain, or conflict we begin to wonder, "Why should I even try? Why should I keep pressing? The only thing I get is more of the same."

Even though you cannot see or feel the evidence of your struggle coming together for your good, it is. Do not be discouraged instead let the negativity that is hurled your way be used to your edification. To be attacked is to be taught and strengthened. So smile, keep it moving, and get your blessing!

BONUS
NEEDED DAILY

DAY 31

"The only way to "Do It" is to just Do It! Stop thinking about it and be about it..."

Do you have a vision and a plan for your life; yet you lack a clear path to get there? Do not be dismayed. Almost every successful person who has pursued greater also had to learn as they went. Despite your occasional lack of clear vision, do not be discouraged. In the moments when the journey becomes too heavy to bear, allow the burning passion of your dream to be the guiding light that helps brighten the sometimes hazy journey ahead. Ideas are just ideas until you execute them. Whether you sink or swim, to do something is better than doing nothing!

No matter the path you choose to take always stay encouraged, motivated, and inspired. At times you will be lost and unsure of which way to turn. Stay on track by focusing on what you can accomplish now versus dwelling on why you can't because of what you need.

Zig Ziglar said it best when he stated that "motivation is like bathing...it's needed every day." So be motivated by something. For encouragement is the stimulus that helps to push you on a day by day basis to continue pursuing what seemed to be the impossible.

MAKE IT A REALITY

DON'T WAIT FOR A MAP! FORGE YOUR OWN PATH TO SUCCESS

After hitting rock bottom and not believing that my life could get any worse or any lower, behold it did. I was faced with the task of rebuilding a life that I no longer wanted to be a part of. After many failed attempts, false starts, and hindering obstacles I began the task of putting my broken life back together. Renewed I was determined to identify why I continued to go through the same broken cycle. Even as I tried to find my place and my purpose in life.

Never stable, I constantly had ideas but, never the drive, the direction or the resources to consistently follow through. Eventually, I took the steps needed to turn my fledgling life around. I became a more attentive mother, grew my relationship with God, and began to love myself which in time shined through my outer. I came to the realization that peace of mind and success is a daily walk. I dropped a few pounds, gained some, and was rewarded with great purpose. Through the journey of rebuilding my life I realized my purpose.

When one is given the opportunity to create positive change in their own life and others by way of the dream, vision, or goal that has impregnated them, it then becomes their responsibility to birth it out into fruition.

What are you waiting for? Will you really allow another year to pass without ever taking any real and consistent action towards making that vision a reality? Will you ever step out on faith? Do you believe in yourself and the vision for your future? Do you truly trust that the Lord will never leave nor forsake you?

Most people are unwilling to pursue their dreams because they feel that there is too much to lose; the house, the car, their possessions. But is financial freedom, peace of mind, independence, or a legacy passed down through generations not worth the risk...

To have faith takes courage, not to mention boldness...There have been times in my life when I was too embarrassed and fearful to take the steps needed to ensure a healthier, happier, and meaningful life for myself. Constantly I was concerned with what others would think of me if I failed. If all you had was a smidgen of faith, by way of these words I tell you that is enough. That is all you need to begin your transformation for a better tomorrow. For the bible states, "If you have faith as a grain of mustard seed ...nothing shall be impossible unto you."

Because you have this book, somewhere inside of you burns the desire to succeed, accomplish, and excel despite the limitations that possibly surrounds you. Never give up on your dream vision or goal. It's never too late to follow your dreams. There will be times when you are stuck in a rut knowing you want more with no idea where to start. The best course of action is to plan in the areas that you can and take action by stepping out there to make it a reality. Do not let anything or anyone discourage you. As long as you believe and keep your faith, if it's within God's will, He will bless it.

Not only do I believe it, I am walking in it. For twelve years of my life, I helped to promote someone else's agenda and vision for their company. Within that period of time my pay, my vacation, my schedule and my life were determined by another without any consideration for my well-being. It was not until I made the massive decision to resign from that place of employment and pursue my dreams fulltime, that I took back control over my life.

Whatever you hope to achieve can happen as long as you have faith, put forth the work, persevere, endure, and never give up. It can and will happen for you.

Say the following aloud:

It is Possible! Whatever I hoped to achieve...It is Possible! Breaking that cycle of _____...It is Possible!

It is achievable, doable, occasionally   difficult but therefore POSSIBLE!

CAN'T GET ENOUGH?

Have your daily Cup of Jo at the touch of your fingertips! Download the free app '**Morning Cup of Jo**' from the Google Play store today!

SHARE YOUR STORY WITH US

Have you obtained some personal success? Why not share it with us?
Don't worry know success is ever to small to share, we want to celebrate with you…

If you have any questions, concerns, or inspiring words, please feel free to contact us at:
PO BOX 504 UNION CITY, GA 30291
CONTACTUS@INSPIRED2PROSPER.COM

IF YOU WOULD LIKE TO FIND OUT MORE INSPIRED2PROSPER, VISIT:
WWW.INSPIRED2PROSPER.COM
WWW.AHLUMBA.COM

YOU CAN ALSO LIKE US ON FACEBOOK:
WWW.FACEBOOK.COM/INSPIRED2PROSPER
WWW.FACEBOOK.COM/AHLUMBAH

YOU CAN ALSO FOLLOW US ON TWITTER:
WWW.TWITTER.COM/I2P_INTL

Morning Cup of Jo

Ahlumba Harris

ABOUT THE AUTHOR

Ahlumba Harris a high school dropout, a college dropout, and a single mother of one who had the fortitude to search for and obtain more despite the mediocrity that tried to contain her. Just like you she constantly seeks to improve her physical, spiritual, and financial wellbeing for she is in a journey to reach her destiny…